Courtesy of Los Angeles County Museum of Art

Sculpture of Hindu gods Vishnu, Shiva, and Brahma – 10th century

Courtesy of National Museum of Vietnamese History (CC BY-SA 3.0)

Statue of boy Buddha rising up from the lotus flower – the lotus represents purity and enlightenment – 14th century

Courtesy of Wikimedia Commons

Portrait of Martin Luther, German theologian and religious reformer who started the Protestant Reformation in 1517 – portrait dated 1528

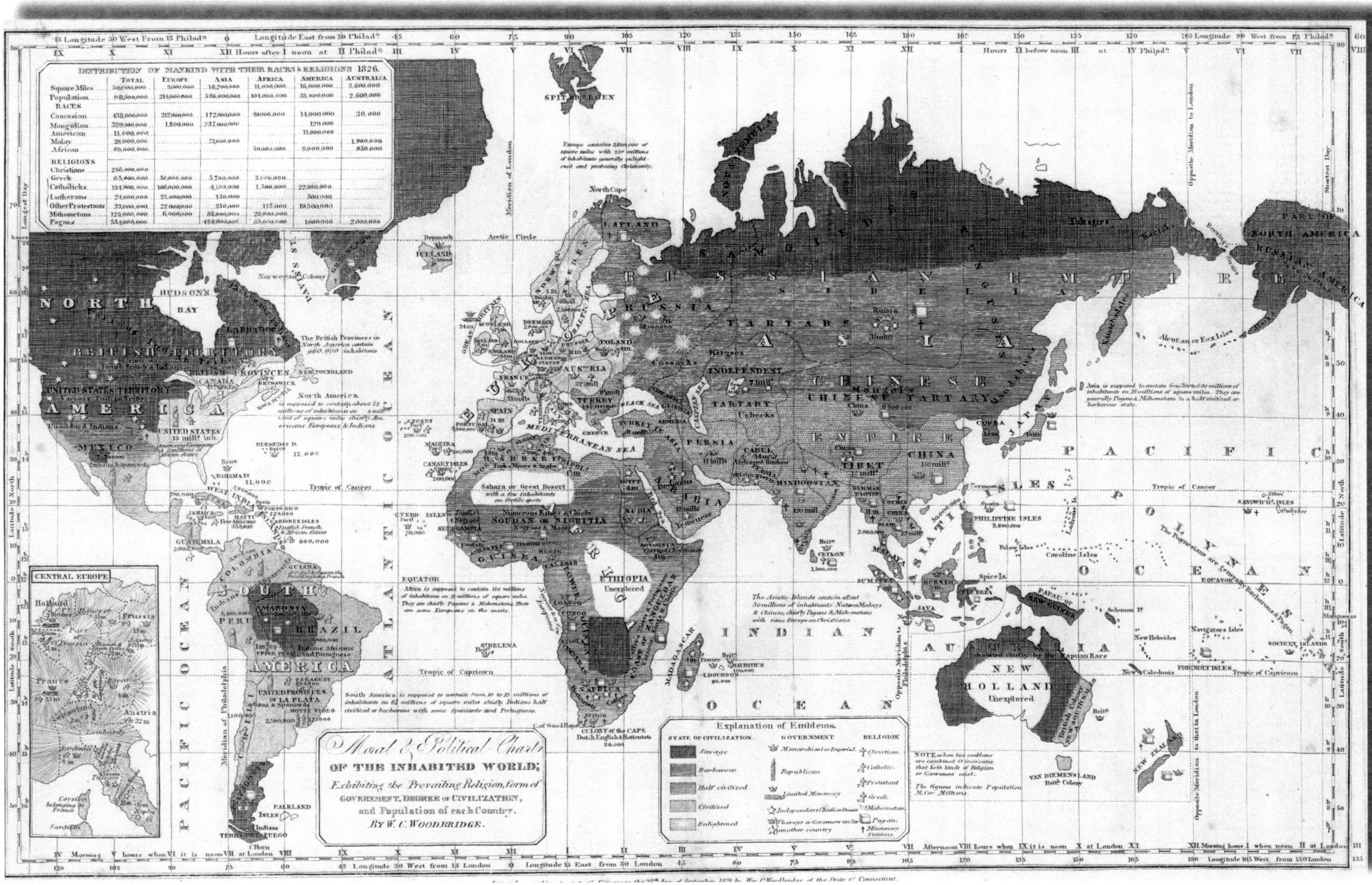

Courtesy of Harvard University Library Virtual Collection

Map of the world, showing how "Christians, Mahometans, and Pagans" correspond to the civilized world – 1821

Courtesy of Wikimedia Commons

Painting depicting Muslim prayer in Cairo, Egypt – 1865

Courtesy of Library of Congress

Photograph showing Muslim washing his feet before prayer – 1865

Courtesy of Wikimedia Commons Courtesy of Tel Aviv Museum of Art

Painting titled *Jews Praying in the Synagogue on Yom Kippur* by Maurycy Gottlieb – holiest day of the year in Judaism – 1878

Courtesy of Library of Congress

Photograph of Hagia Eirene, Greek Eastern Orthodox Church in Istanbul, Turkey – the first church commissioned by Roman emperor Constantine I in Constantinople – photo circa 1900

Courtesy of *The Catholic Altar Boy*

Painting depicting ordination to the priesthood in the Roman Catholic religion – 1922

Courtesy of U.S. Navy

Photograph of U.S. Navy chaplain preparing to baptize a soldier in Iraq – baptism is a religious rite in the Christian religion – 2004

Photograph of a 65-foot-tall concrete statue of the Hindu deity Shiva in Bangalore, India – 2006

Courtesy of David Shankbone (CC BY-SA 3.0)

A Jewish man praying at the Western Wall in Jerusalem, Israel – 2009

Courtesy of Wikimedia Commons

1. torii (gate)
2. stone stairs
3. sandō (visiting path)
4. chōzuya (water purification pavilion)
5. tōrō (traditional lantern)
6. kagura-den (stage used for sacred dance)
7. shamusho (administration office)
8. ema (display area for wooden plaques with prayers or wishes written on them)
9. sessha/massha (miniature shrines)
10. komainu (guardian statues)
11. haiden (worship hall)
12. tamagaki (fence)
13. honden (sanctuary; most sacred place)

Illustration of layout of a Shinto shrine – 2009

Photograph of children studying the Quran in Senegal – 2006

Photograph of St. Peter's Basilica in Vatican City – a symbol of the Catholic church and the largest church in the world – 2006

Courtesy of U.S. Department of Defense

Photograph of Afghan army general (center) with a group of female Afghan National Police members – all women wear hijabs – 2012

Courtesy of Nirmal Dulal (CC BY-SA 3.0)

Photograph of Hindu bride in Nepal – she wears traditional dress, jewelry, and body art – 2012

Courtesy of Wikimedia Commons (CC BY-SA 4.0)

Photograph of statue of the Yellow and Red Gods in Henan Province, China – the Han Chinese claim to be descendants of these gods – 2013

Photograph of young Buddhist monks in Cambodia – 2013

Courtesy of Aviral Sanghera (CC BY 3.0)

Photograph of Sikhs visiting their most revered temple, the Golden Temple in Punjab, India – 2017